BUILDING PERSONAL
EFFECTIVENESS FOR
PROFESSIONAL SUCCESS

Better Management Skills

This highly popular range of inexpensive paperbacks covers all areas of basic management. Practical, easy to read and instantly accessible, these guides will help managers to improve their business or communication skills. Those marked * are available on audio cassette.

The books in this series can be tailored to specific company requirements. For further details, please contact the publisher, Kogan Page, telephone 0171 278 0433, fax 0171 837 6348.

Be a Successful Supervisor
Be Positive
Building High Performance Teams
Business Creativity
Business Ethics
Business Etiquette
Coaching Your Employees
Conducting Effective Interviews
Counselling Your Staff
Creating a Learning Organisation
Creative Decision-making
Creative Thinking in Business
Delegating for Results
Develop Your Assertiveness
Effective Business Briefings
Effective Employee Participation
Effective Meeting Skills
Effective Networking for
  Professional Success
Effective Performance Appraisals*
Effective Presentation Skills
Empowering People
Empowerment
Facilitation Skills for Team
  Development
First Time Supervisor
Get Organised!
Goals and Goal Setting
How to Communicate Effectively*
How to Develop a Positive
  Attitude*
How to Manage Organisational Change
How to Motivate People*
How to Plan Your Competitive
  Strategy
How to Reward Your Staff
How to Understand Financial
  Statements
How to Write a Marketing Plan
How to Write a Staff Manual

Improving Relations at Work
Keeping Customers for Life
Leadership Skills for Women
Learning to Lead
Making TQM Work
Managing Cultural Diversity at Work
Managing Disagreement
  Constructively
Managing Employee Stress
Managing Organisational
  Change
Managing Part-time Employees
Managing Quality Customer
  Service
Managing Your Boss
Marketing for Success
Memory Skills in Business
Mentoring
NLP for Business Success
Office Management
Organisation Design
Personnel Testing
Process Improvement
Project Management from
  Idea to Implementation
Quality Customer Service for
  Front Line Staff
Rate Your Skills as a Manager
Sales Training Basics
Self-managing Teams
Selling Professionally
Successful Negotiation
Successful Presentation Skills
Successful Telephone Techniques
Systematic Problem-solving and
  Decision-making
Team Building
Training Methods that Work
The Internal Consultant
The Woman Manager

BUILDING PERSONAL EFFECTIVENESS FOR PROFESSIONAL SUCCESS

A FIVE-POINT PLAN TO IMPROVE YOUR PRODUCTIVITY AND ACHIEVE YOUR GOALS

PAUL R TIMM

KOGAN PAGE
BETTER MANAGEMENT SKILLS

First published in the United States of America in 1997, entitled *Successful Self-management*, by Crisp Publications Inc, 1200 Hamilton Court, Menlo Park, California 94025, USA.

This edition first published in Great Britain in 1998 by Kogan Page Ltd, 120 Pentonville Road, London N1 9JN.

British Library Cataloguing in Publication Data

A CIP record for this book is available from the British Library.

ISBN 0-7494-2717-5

Typeset by BookEns Ltd, Royston, Herts.
Printed in England by Clays Ltd, St Ives plc

Contents

About this Book

Building Personal Effectiveness for Professional Success is not like most books. It stands out from other self-help books in an important way. It's not a book to read – it's a book to *use.* The unique 'self-paced' format of this book and the many worksheets, encourage a reader to get involved and try some new ideas immediately.

This book will introduce the critical building blocks of self-management which ultimately determine our personal and professional success. Using the simple yet sound techniques presented can make a dramatic change in one's productivity, accomplishments and life satisfaction.

Building Personal Effectiveness for Professional Success can be used effectively in a number of ways. Here are some possibilities:

- *Individual study.* Because the book is self-instructional, all that is needed is a quiet place, some time and a pencil. By completing the activities and exercises, a reader should not only receive valuable feedback, but also practical steps for self-improvement.
- *Workshops and seminars.* The book is ideal for assigned reading prior to a workshop or seminar. With the basics in hand, the quality of the participation will improve, and more time can be spent on concept extensions and applications during the programme. The book is also effective when it is distributed at the beginning of a session, and participants 'work through' the contents.

- *Remote location training.* Books can be sent to those not able to attend 'home office' training sessions.

There are several other possibilities that depend on the objectives, programme or ideas of the user.

Finally, this book provides master forms that may be photocopied for personal use. These forms will get the reader started on applying the skills needed for successful self-management.

One thing's for sure, even after it has been read, this book will be looked at — and thought about — again and again.

Preface to this Revised Edition

In the six years since I wrote *Successful Self-management* (now retitled *Building Personal Effectiveness for Professional Success*), I've seen countless examples of people experiencing new levels of personal growth and life satisfaction by applying these ideas. These people are breaking away from the 'do more, do better and do it faster' mentality that had them running like racehorses around a track that had no finish line.

From the millionaire computer executive who finds a new level of joy in teaching at a community college to the lawyer who turns to woodworking or the homemaker who launches his or her own business, people are reaching their own conclusions on the definition of success. Life, they are finding, is much more than reacting to the world's demands.

Success is being defined in a broader, more intelligent way. It is not what the world defines it to be. It is internally based and highly individual.

Regardless of one's definition of success, getting there is no accident. It is a process of self-management. This book provides a sensible, logical and psychologically sound way to master self-management. With the skills you'll learn in this book, you will enjoy the thrill of the chase and the joy of reaching inner contentment that tells you that you are much more than a modern day racehorse. You are a person of enormous worth and potential.

Making the most of that potential may well be a matter of applying the keys to successful self-management. So let's get to it.

Preface to Original Edition

'Do more, do better and *do it faster!*' If we were to build a statue honouring modern society, that could be the inscription. The statue itself should be a racehorse — with blinkers. Fast and strong, but without the faintest idea where it's going. And after running as hard as it can, the horse ends up back where it started.

Do you sometimes feel like such an animal? You've trained, and you're ready to run for the finishing line, but you're not sure where the track is?

Most bookstores are loaded with titles on how to achieve that siren Goddess: '*success*' or how to achieve that management buzz-word: '*excellence*'. But there is much the experts fail to tell us about the thrill of the chase, and the joy of reaching the inner contentment that tells you that you really are a person of worth, not another modern-day racehorse.

There are things we can do to take charge of our success. This book teaches skills of human effectiveness common to all achievers. These include understanding control, focusing your purpose, using key personality attributes, planning for time and task management, boosting personal productivity and maintaining balance amid conflicting demands.

So take your blinkers off, and jump the rail. You're in for the time of your life as you master the keys to successful self-management.

Paul R Timm, PhD

CHAPTER 1
Getting Started

Where are you now?

The following assessment has been designed to assist you in getting started on the path to improved self-management. It is essential that you answer each question honestly. Since *Building Personal Effectiveness for Professional Success* was designed as a 'do-it-yourself' book, the only person affected by your answers and actions is you!

1. Do you have a clear picture of where you are going with your professional life in the next five years? ☐ yes ☐ no
2. Do others (ie your supervisor/subordinates) know about your plans? ☐ yes ☐ no
3. Have you set specific targets for your personal life for the next five years? ☐ yes ☐ no
4. Do those you count on for support (family, close friends, etc) know about these targets? ☐ yes ☐ no
5. Are you totally satisfied with the progress you are making in your professional life? ☐ yes ☐ no
6. Are you satisfied with your personal life progress? ☐ yes ☐ no

7. Do you have a written method to track
    your professional and personal progress? ☐ yes ☐ no
8. Are your underlying values clear and
    sharp in your mind? ☐ yes ☐ no
9. Have you written them down? ☐ yes ☐ no
10. Do you sometimes feel guilty about
    successes you have? ☐ yes ☐ no
11. Are you as successful as you can be? ☐ yes ☐ no

Self-management defined

Your answers to the questions on page 13 can help pinpoint opportunities for self-management improvement. The rest of this book is designed to help you convert these 'opportunities' for improvement into reality.

An acceptable definition of self-management would be:

Self-management is the *process* of maximizing our *time* and *talents* to achieve *worthwhile goals* based on a sound *value system.*

Note the key words in this definition:

Process: Self-management is ongoing. It is not something we do only once or occasionally. We make it a process by adopting some simple 'rituals' which will be taught in this book.
Time and *talents*: These are unique personal resources which we alone can manage. In essence, this is all we have to offer and can really manage.
Worthwhile goals: These are the outcomes of our efforts – our planned-for achievements. To be truly worth while, such goals must be rooted in a sound value system.
Value system: Ultimately, we move towards that which we value. Understanding our *personal* values is critical to the process of self-management.

As you work through this book, you will be taught the required skills to make the above definition of self-management a natural part of your life. In so doing, you will achieve even greater heights of psychological comfort and life satisfaction.

CHAPTER 2
Five Building Blocks to Success

This chapter will describe five 'building blocks'. Understanding and applying these concepts will allow you to develop the self-management skills necessary to become a more effective and confident person.

The five building blocks are:

Block 1 – understanding perspective

Perspective is our attitude about the amount of control we have over our lives. Some people feel helpless and overwhelmed by the demands the world seems to place upon them. Other people act as if they have virtually total *control* over every event that might effect them.

Let's think for a moment about this issue of personal control. I remember the first time I went skiing. My wife and I, both newcomers to the sport, visited a beautiful Utah ski resort with friends. After an hour of slipping around feeling awkward, our friends Dave and Judy patiently explained the basics (ie how to stand up on skis and create the illusion that you've done all this before). Finally they announced it was time for our first lift ride.

It took only a few moments on the lift for a terrifying realization to enter my mind. I noticed the lift seats were coming back down the mountain — empty. I also deduced that the lift never stopped to let people off! That meant that like it or not we were going to have to *ski* off the top of a mountain (to certain death, I was sure). The sinking feeling that we had given up control pushed us way outside our comfort zone. It was scary.

Some people feel they have no control over any aspects of their lives. They see themselves as helplessly floating on a sea of waves and currents. They resign themselves to drifting and that's exactly what they do throughout their lives.

Other people have unrealistic views of what they can control. They think that they have more power than they do and get very frustrated when people or events fail to yield to their control efforts.

Psychologists classify people according to their 'locus of control'.* Some have an *external* locus meaning that they see the outside world as controlling them. Others have an *internal* locus meaning that they feel they have a lot of control over what happens to them. An internal locus of control is needed for self-management although it must be tempered by reality. We are all subject to some external forces over which we have no control, but much in our life can be influenced by us.

Like my wife and me on skis, we sometimes place ourselves in situations where we no longer hold control. Children do this at amusement parks. They eagerly hop on scary rides. The more threatening the name of the ride, the better. The Maniacal Rodent, Terror Mountain, The Bone Crusher — they love them all. Other people when cajoled into riding one of

---

* The term 'locus' means place, locality or source.

these things, can think only of every possible way the ride could crash and catch fire. They hate giving up control even for a few minutes.

Although these conservative people may miss out on some of the fun, they take comfort in avoiding out-of-control feelings. In life, most of us grind against feelings of no control. In fact, a major source of occupational stress arises from having too little control on the job.

Off the job, people increasingly find themselves adding the number of balls they are trying to juggle. Career, family, civic or religious activities, physical fitness education and other self-improvement efforts all take a bite out of our precious time and drain our limited energy. This coupled with a 'do more, do better' mindset places considerable pressure on people. This is why many of us feel that our lives are out of control.

How do you look at control?

In the left column of the box below, list some events or activities which may affect your life, over which you have *no control*. (Typical items may be the weather or the stock market.) In the right column, list events or activities that you *can control*. Finally, list some events or activities that fit somewhere in between, in the grey area. These are things you may have *some* control over.

Events or activities that		
I cannot control	**Grey area**	**I can control**

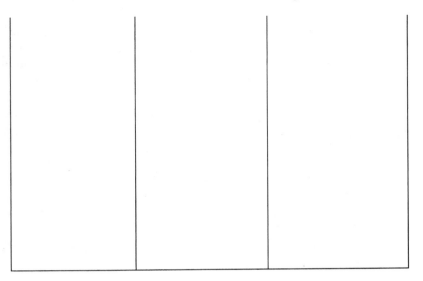

Do you see any common characteristics in the items listed above? Most people find that there are several things they cannot control and many of them have to do with *other people*. The activities in our lives that we can control usually have to do with *ourselves*. This leads to the simple conclusion that:

The most fertile area for greater control lies within ourselves

For most events in life we can have some influence — but seldom will we have ultimate control. This applies especially to our dealings with other people.

A healthy perspective towards life control may be summarized this way:

- Life is a never-ending series of demands upon our time and efforts. This 'stream' is constantly fed by bosses, sub-ordinates, family, friends, our sense of obligation and our basic needs.
- For the successful self-manager — one who tries to maximize control of his or her own life — the stream is also fed by clearly determined goals, aspirations and values.

- Look at who is feeding your stream. Then take control by choosing to respond to those demands that best meet your true needs. Herein lies the first key to successful self-management.

Self-quiz: how you allocate your time and talents

Tick yes or no beside each of the following statements to reflect how you act *as a general rule*. Be honest; don't show your answers to others.

1. I spend most of my day doing what other people want me to do. ☐ yes ☐ no
2. I work on fun or pleasant tasks before doing the unpleasant ones. ☐ yes ☐ no
3. I wait until a deadline is near before really getting to work on a project. ☐ yes ☐ no
4. I give a high priority to those tasks that will advance by personal goals. ☐ yes ☐ no
5. I tackle jobs that can be completed in a short time before working on larger, longer-term tasks. ☐ yes ☐ no
6. I do the work which I've planned before doing the unexpected. ☐ yes ☐ no
7. I tackle the small jobs before embarking on the bigger ones. ☐ yes ☐ no
8. I work on the squeaky-wheel principle – the task that 'makes the most noise' gets worked on first. ☐ yes ☐ no
9. I wait to be told what to do first. ☐ yes ☐ no
10. I regularly think about how I am expending my efforts relative to my personal goals. ☐ yes ☐ no

Self-quiz results
The self-quiz above may tell you something about your perspective on control.

If you answered yes to items 1, 3, 8 or 9 you tend to be *reactive* to outside demand. You wait until someone (or someone's deadline) pushes you into action.

If you answered yes to items 2, 5 or 7, you may be acting upon *mistaken priorities.* Your decision to work on something appears to be because it looks easy or can be done quickly. People who do this regularly find themselves tangled in the trivial and seldom seem to have time or energy for what may be much more important.

If you answered yes to items 4, 6 or 10, you are showing a *proactive* stance and are more likely in control. Saying yes to these questions means you are moving towards successful life-management.

To be proactive is good, providing that you know where you are going. This brings us to our second success building block: *purpose* which is described in the next section.

Block 2 – understanding purpose

Our second success building block is *purpose.* People without a strong sense of purpose lack focus in their lives. They are often guilty of living by wandering around (LBWA), which may the single most common cause of poor self-management.

Focus adds power to our actions. If somebody throws a bucket of water on you, you'd get wet, and probably get mad. But if water was shot at you through a high-pressure nozzle you might get injured.

Similarly, the 'trick' to karate is that the entire force of a blow is centred in a very small area like the edge of the hand. That's why black-belt karate experts can slam through a stack of boards with no pain. They are *focused.* No mental or physical 'wandering around' here. The karate user's mind and body is totally concentrated, and the results are stunning.

Gaining focus with value clarification or letting your deeply-held beliefs guide your life

When Tom Peters, author of the well-known book *In Search of Excellence*, is asked for 'one, all-purpose bit of advice' which will help organizations achieve excellence, he responds:

> Figure out your value system. Decide what your company stands for ... Put yourself out 20 years in the future: What would you look back on with the greatest satisfaction?

The same advice holds for individuals. Melanie Brown explains in *Attaining Personal Greatness* that 'the real distinction between being great and being less great seems to be the extent to which we are willing to be pushed along *by our own best desires* [emphasis added].' Clarifying and articulating these deepest desires isn't easy. If it were, more people would do it. It takes mental effort and some clear thinking. But once articulated, these true desires become the personal values that form the basis of successful self-management. This defines our life's purposes.

A value is a concept of the desirable — an idea that is, in and of itself, alluring. To make it a personal value simply add the words 'to me'. Clarifying a value system, for organizations *and* for individuals, is a powerful idea. Leading companies are aware of its power and we should be, too.

Your personal values need not be validated by popular vote. They don't have to agree with what other people think is valuable. They are uniquely yours. (Obviously if your value is counter to what society values, you may meet some resistance. If you value, for example, armed robbery as an expedient way to make a living, you'll pay a price for running against the norm.)

But on a more positive note, once our value system is clarified, it will provide focus for our lives. By contrast, less effective people and organizations are typically marked by no coherent set of deeply-held beliefs. They tend to look only at results that can be easily measured — *quantity* goals. They count how many of something they produce or sell, for example.

Value-guided people and companies, on the other hand, express their deeply-held beliefs in *quality* terms like customer satisfaction, innovation, personal growth, self-esteem and life satisfaction.

The most important work of any leader is to clarify and breathe life into a value system. Once articulated, this system provides a mission statement for leaders and followers alike.

How can we identify our value system? An effective way to begin is provided in the worksheet in the next section.

Values worksheet

Mark each of the values listed below in one of the following ways:

- Put a tick mark next to those values you personally espouse or champion. These values you would be *willing to dedicate significant time and energy to achieve.*
- Put an X beside those values that you personally reject. These are values you would *not* be willing to expend much time or effort to achieve.
- Put a 0 beside those values that are neutral to you — you neither espouse nor reject these.

Many of the values below will probably sound good to you. Force yourself to make some choices. Be honest about your willingness to dedicate a significant amount of time or effort to each. Do not show your responses to anyone.

I value ...

- career success
- honesty in all my dealings
- religious activity
- social correctness
- open-mindedness
- high individualism
- winning
- my family's success
- giving my children a competitive advantage ☐

- ☐ financial wealth ☐
- self-sufficiency ☐
- ☐ involvement in government ☐
- ☐ marital harmony ☐
- ☐ fame within my profession ☐
- ☐ being productive ☐
- ☐ being creative ☐
- serving the less fortunate ☐

- health and vigour
- being law-abiding
- being loyal to country
- orderly home life
- keeping all commitments ☐
- knowing the right people
- having balance in my life
- having a wide range of friends
- having many skills
- being prepared for emergencies
- athletic excellence
- pride in my community, state, region
- musical excellence
- awareness of my heritage
- projecting the right image
- honouring my parents

☐● ability to build things ☐
☐● habits of thrift ☐
☐● accuracy of work ☐
☐● strong discipline ☐
☐● financial security ☐
● personal attractiveness ☐
☐● tolerance of others ☐
● being witty, clever, ☐ articulate
● artistic sensitivity ☐
☐● being a good team ☐ player
● dressing for success ☐
☐● skill to influence ☐
☐● skill to repair things or solve problems ☐
☐● keeping careful records ☐
☐● understanding other cultures — diversity ☐
☐● being a leader ☐
● mentoring others ☐
☐● intellectual growth ☐
☐● trust in God ☐

Now rank in order the four values you endorse most strongly and the four values you reject most vigorously:

My top four espoused values: *My top four rejected values:*

1. _____   1. _____

2. _____   2. _____

3. _____   3. _____

4. _____   4. _____

The value worksheet is designed to start you thinking about

values. Review your list of the top four values you support and four you reject most strongly.

- Do you spend a major portion of your productive time moving towards agreement with your top four values? ☐ yes ☐ no
- Do you spend time and effort moving towards achievement of values you *reject*? ☐ yes ☐ no

In the box below, identify one value conflict you noticed from this exercise. Can you pinpoint areas where you are now spending too much time and effort? Are there other areas where you should be doing more? Suggest an action you could take to achieve better alignment with what you truly value.

Further value sharpening

This section contains another exercise that can help you begin to focus on your core values. Take a few minutes to answer these questions, bearing in mind that your responses will be just a rough draft. Then come back to these at another time and see if your answers still hold. Core values hold up to the test of time.

1. What would you best want to be remembered for? What will your obituary say about you when you have finished this life?

   _____

   _____

2. What are your most important goals for this year?

   _____

   _____

   _____

3. What are your major professional and personal goals for the next year? (Name two or three in each category.) For the next five years?

   _____

   _____

   _____

4. Twenty years from now
   - where will you live?

   _____

   _____

   - what will you be doing?

   _____

   _____

   - what assets will you own?

   _____

   _____

- what abilities will you have mastered?

_____

_____

- how will you spend your time?

_____

_____

5. If you had all the money you wanted, what would you do with your time? (Be specific.)

_____

_____

_____

6. If you knew that you would die in one year, what would you want to accomplish?

_____

_____

_____

More thoughts on value clarification

Values are crucial to personal excellence
Personal effectiveness and balance require us to hold a set of clear personal values. Without such deeply-held beliefs, we are much more likely to gallop off in different directions according to whim. Without values, self-management becomes little more than choosing from an array of equally worthy (or unworthy) activities. Without values, we become subject to 'the tyranny of the immediate', and react to events rather than doing that which is most meaningful to us.

It isn't easy to sort out our values
If value clarification were an easy process, more people would do it. But it isn't and they don't. One reason for the difficulty of the task is that values often present conflicts between two desirable goods.

For example, a worker may feel a need to maintain friendships by socializing with co-workers, but this could conflict with the need to get away from others and finish a task. Another difficult choice may be the question of allowing children (or inexperienced workers) the freedom to made personal choices, which can result in the high cost of their mistakes due to inexperience.

Once values are clear, people reduce the need to make uncomfortable choices. Their behaviour is spontaneously 'right' — consistent with their values.

Value clarification must be put to work
Careful value planning takes time. This book will get you started, but the greatest benefit will come to those who spend hours on the *process* of value shaping.

One systematic way to do this is to set up a notebook or planner that provides a place to write your core values and related activities.

The three-step value shaping process
Using a 'Life Plan Worksheet' similar to the one found in the *Plan-it Life Organizer*, let's work through an example of value clarification. Write your value shaping exercise (Figure 2.3) on page 31 as you work through this exercise.

First, name the value. Give it a name that you feel comfortable with. A good value area might be called 'health and vigour'. Others could be 'financial security', 'family', 'leadership', 'personal success', 'spiritual growth' or 'balance'. Use terms that are meaningful to you. (The activity referred to on page 23 shows many other possible names.)

Next, write the name of one value on your Life Plan Worksheet in the left column (see page 29), and after you have written the named value, *describe*, using the present tense, what it will be like when this value becomes a reality in your life — when you are living in agreement with that value. An example using 'health and vigour' as a value is illustrated in Figure 2.1.

plan·it life organizer	Life Plan
✓ **Core Values**	**Value Aligning Activities**
HEALTH AND VIGOUR	
✓ exercise regularly and avoid harmful habits. I maintain reasonable weight. I get regular medical and dental check ups. I maintain vigour by daily planning, goal-setting, and rewarding myself for accomplishments. I jog, play squash, swim, play golf, and occasionally do wild and crazy things to let off steam. I refuse to let stress grind me down. I avoid excessive worry. I view life as fun and full of opportunity	• Jog 1000+ miles this year • Get medical physical every 2 years • Have eyes checked every 3 years

Figure 2.1   *The three-step value shaping process — health and vigour*

Although the figure shows all those descriptors in the present tense, it is not necessary to have achieved them all yet. For example, no one is always able to avoid stress or excessive worry, and perhaps some activities (such as golf) are not regularly played. But putting descriptors in the present tense indicates the direction that a person wants to go.

Here's another example (Figure 2.2), using the value heading 'financial security':

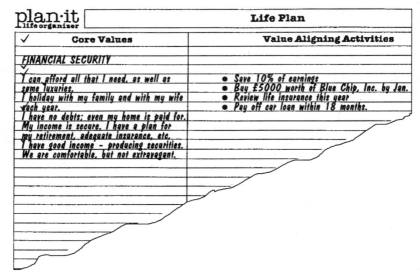

Figure 2.2 *The three-step value shaping process — financial security*

The following summarizes the three steps in basic value shaping:

1. name the value
2. describe what it feels like to have this value as a reality in your life
3. describe value aligning activities (these are covered in the next section.)

plan·it _{life organiser}	**Life Plan**
Core Values	**Value Aligning Activities**

Figure 2.3 *A value shaping exercise*

plan·it life organizer	Life Plan
Core Values	**Value Aligning Activities**

Figure 2.3   *(continued)*

Value aligning activities: the comfortable marriage of values and goals

Too often people oversimplify setting goals. They confuse goal-setting with wishing or daydreaming. It is much more than that. Goals rooted in clear values are the bedrock of any success programme.

Much has been written about goal-setting. We have all heard the familiar litany: set short- and long-term goals, concentrate on them really hard, direct your energies towards their accomplishment and you will have *success!*

Goal-setting is a motivational technique that works — it is not a fad. As one textbook which surveyed the research on goal-setting concludes, 'In business and in life, goal-setting is a uniquely powerful tool for increasing productivity.'

But why does it work? It works because goals give direction to life. They provide points of reference.

This book differs from many other goal-setting books because it maintains that *at the base of any goal must lie an anchoring value.* Understanding the *value* adds power to the goal.

If an individual sets goals, for example, to do the following:

1. jog 20 miles each week
2. take each of the children out for a 'date' this month, and
3. make 125 sales calls this month

what might be the underlying values? Write your answers in the spaces below.

1. _____

2. _____

3. _____

Author's comments

The jogging goal would probably be anchored in some value called health; the 'date with the children' goal would be based in a value having to do with family; and the sales call goal probably finds its root in a career value.

But goals often relate to several, interconnected values. The sales call goal can be based on financial, personal growth or even social values.

A personal value system can be visualized as the foundation of a building. The goals and activities will be structurally sound only to the extent that the foundation is solid.

Failure to create a linkage between goals and their values runs the risk of working towards goals which have no permanent attachment to personal values. Such goals are hollow.

Characteristics of good goals

Effective goals — the kind that really do motivate — should be:

- *concrete and specific* — phrased in a way that is clear
- *realistic* — they should stretch us, but not beyond the bounds of what is reasonable
- *measurable in some way* — either we can count them (eg, the number of miles run or items sold) or we can feel their accomplishment (eg, reduced nervousness before people or more attention paid to the childrens' needs)
- *deadline-targeted*
- *value-anchored*
- *written* — an unrecorded goal is only a wish.

Go back to the Life Plan Worksheets on pages 31 and 32 (Figure 2.3). In the column to the right of the 'core value' is a place to write your 'value aligning activities'. For each value you have described on the worksheet, write several such action targets which will help you achieve alignment with your value.

For example, next to the 'health and vigour' value on page 29 (Figure 2.1), the individual has written that he or she will jog at least 1000 miles per year, get a complete physical examination every two years and have his or her eyes checked every three years.

In similar fashion, the 'financial security' value example on page 30 (Figure 2.2) is accompanied by the following activities: save 10 per cent of earnings; buy £5000 worth of Blue Chip, Inc. stock by January; review life insurance coverage every three years and pay off car loan within 18 months.

Every goal-seeking activity in the above examples is anchored in a value. The value clarification process helps to make purposeful goals, and these goals provide the motivation to achieve success.

Herein lies the productive marriage of values and goals.

If it isn't written it isn't a goal

People in my seminars often say, 'I have lots of goals, I just haven't written them down.' My reaction is: if a goal isn't written, it isn't a goal — it's a wish. Occasionally wishes come true, but not as often as goals.

The power of goals lies in the ways they plant ideas in the mind. To do so requires repetition. Repeated ideas reinforce the direction to go. Reading written goals provides the repetition.

Block 3 – understanding your personality

The third building block is *personality*. While many aspects of personality can affect one's success, two aspects have the greatest impact:

1. assertiveness
2. receptiveness.

Assertiveness

Assertiveness and aggressiveness are often confused. They are different. An excellent definition of assertiveness is *being pleasantly direct*. You need not be aggressive or pushy to be assertive. In fact, assertiveness creates none of the adverse reactions that aggressiveness or pushiness may do.

Assertiveness calls into play the building blocks we've

already discussed. With an understanding of *control* (Block 1), a clearer *value system* and *focused goals* (Block 2), you are now ready to make better decisions about the use of your time and talents. When faced with requests (or demands) to do something that runs against your plan, you'll have ammunition you need to say the most important word in the self-manager's vocabulary: *no.*

With assertiveness, you will do so in a pleasantly direct manner.

How assertive are you?

By honestly answering the following questions, you can get an idea of your attitudes toward assertiveness. An attitude, of course, does not always show up in behaviours. You may feel more assertive than you are in real-life situations.

Circle T (true) or F (false):

1. I often feel like telling people what I really think of them.   T F
2. When I find myself in a new situation, I watch what other people do and then try to act the same as they do.   T F
3. I like to do things that others may regard as unconventional.   T F
4. I think it is important to learn obedience and correct social behaviour.   T F
5. In general, I find that I dislike non-conformists.   T F
6. I prefer to listen to other people's opinions before I take a stand.   T F
7. I like to follow instructions and do what is expected of me.   T F
8. It often makes more sense to go along with 'the group' rather than try to persuade them to accept my point of view.   T F
9. Confronting people is extremely uncomfortable for me.   T F
10. I enjoy being seen as a person with strong opinions.   T F

Scoring your assertiveness quiz

If you answered true to items 2, 4, 5, 6, 7, 8 or 9, give yourself one point for each. Also give one point for false answers to items 1, 3 or 10. Total your points.

If you scored 6 or more points, low assertiveness may be a problem for you. You may find yourself being far more reactive to the demands of others than you are to your own aspirations.

Many excellent books are available that can help develop one's assertiveness. Read some of this material and try on some new, more assertive behaviour.

How receptive are you?

Receptiveness means fishing for feedback
Getting feedback, even from your most severe critic, may be the most important way of gaining the direction and control that leads to better self-management.

CASE STUDY

While jogging together one afternoon, Terry and Marie got on the subject of corrective criticism. Terry confided that he was having some difficulty understanding why his career didn't seem to be going anywhere. He sensed that his boss wasn't very supportive — she didn't seem to care if he succeeded or not.

'If only she'd say what it is about me that doesn't appeal to her, I'd work on changing. But she just won't say.'

'That can be frustrating,' Marie agreed. 'Maybe she's just uncomfortable telling you what bugs her.'

'You're an old friend, Marie. What do you think I'm doing wrong?'

Marie thought for a moment: Terry is a really good guy, but he does have some irritating behaviour. For example, he's extremely competitive. So what the heck, she thought, I'll tell him now while he seems to be looking for feedback.

'Terry,' she began, 'You do have one behavioural trait that I find irritating and maybe it bugs your boss too. You are the most bloodthirsty, competitive person I've ever met.' Terry didn't say anything at first. In fact, he didn't see any inaccuracy in her statement, although she worded it pretty harshly.

In fact, Marie was warming up to this and Terry didn't seem too upset by what she'd just said, so she went on: 'In fact, I notice whenever we play squash, it isn't even fun. You're so damn intense, you won't even say "nice shot" when I hit a winner. To be honest with you, Terry, you'd be a lot nicer guy to be around if you'd be a little more charitable with your compliments — a bit better at the old sportsmanship.'

She was on a roll now: 'In fact, Terry, I'd much rather play squash with Brent. Every game doesn't seem like life or death to him. He just has fun. And he's a nicer guy than you and he's forever saying "great shot" and he's still a friend after the game even if I beat him and he even lets up once in a while if I'm having a miserable game and ...'

Suddenly, it sunk in that Terry wasn't responding. He wasn't getting mad and he wasn't even thoughtfully considering this 'constructive criticism'. Actually he was laughing out loud. Marie found that disconcerting, until he explained:

'Marie, do you realize that you just described perfectly, *your* style on the squash court? That's exactly why I get frustrated playing against *you*.'

Marie wanted to give him her best 'Oh yeah, says who ...' when a large light-bulb went on over her head. He was right. She did do those things. Of course, she was just reacting to him. He started it!

After a moment, she started laughing too. He was right, of course. She was taking the game too seriously. But the exchange really was instructive. They both got some useful feedback and their friendship was strengthened by it.

Author's comments on Terry and Marie's conversation
Let's look at what happened between Terry and Marie. First, Terry asked for feedback from a trusted friend. That's

receptiveness and it can be healthy. The story also illustrated that receptiveness can reveal interesting, and sometimes unexpected, information about both the participants. Both Terry and Marie learnt something about their behaviour as observed by the other.

What they each might choose to do with that information is up to them. In the interest of self-management growth, I would suggest that each has received a gift of a fresh perspective — a new look — at the way they may be coming across to others. This story also illustrates that sometimes receptiveness gets you information you didn't even ask for (and might not be all that eager to hear).

Feedback receptiveness quiz

Answer as honestly as possible. As a general rule:

1. I get embarrassed when people point out my mistakes. ☐ yes ☐ no
2. I resent people who tell me what they think of my shortcomings. ☐ yes ☐ no
3. I regularly ask trusted associates to comment on how I'm doing. ☐ yes ☐ no
4. I offer constructive criticism to others in a sensitive way without hurting their feelings. ☐ yes ☐ no
5. I like people who tell me how they react to my actions because it helps me do better. ☐ yes ☐ no

Author's comments on feedback receptiveness
If you answered a strong yes to items 1 and 2 you may be putting up some attitude barriers that could deter you from getting useful feedback.

We are all somewhat uncomfortable when we receive harsh or insensitive feedback, but even that can be valuable — if we take it in our stride. Even our worst critic can give us a gift of good advice, if we don't allow the emotion of the moment to blind us.

Work to develop an attitude of searching for that gem of good advice, even it it's buried under a lot of worthless dirt.

If you answered yes to items 3 and 4 you are helping to create a climate where helpful feedback is accepted and expected.

Organizations with such a climate typically prosper. Likewise, individuals who foster an attitude of being 'teachable' receive the benefit of the input of others.

If you answered a strong yes to item 5, you are probably a little unusual.

But you're on the right track.

We never really do know how we are coming across to others unless we ask — unless we seek some feedback. Feedback: the breakfast of champions — and a critical ingredient in successful self-management.

Feedback in business

Why an unhappy 'customer' can be your best friend
Feedback is critical to an effective business. Customer service studies indicate that dissatisfied customers tell, on average, 11 other people about a bad service experience. Almost a quarter of unhappy customers tell 20 or more people. Studies also show that it costs five times as much to gain a new customer than it does to keep an existing one.

Another interesting fact is that most dissatisfied customers who receive some 'adjustment' from the business do come back. The most dangerous situation is to have unhappy customers *not* tell the company of their dissatisfaction. In a sense, an unhappy customer is a company's best friend *if the company gets feedback*. Because of this, enlightened companies go to great lengths to make it easy for customers to complain.

Feedback receptiveness is an attitude. Less successful companies and people prefer to be ostriches. They bury their heads in the sand and tune out any negative comments. But they leave one end exposed!

Confirming and clarifying how we are coming across to others requires getting feedback from those we deal with. Feedback becomes the control system of our self-management.

Have the courage to ask, 'What am I doing that's stupid?' (Well, maybe you'll want to phrase that a little differently, but you get the idea.)

Complete the following sentence in your own words:

I plan to encourage useful feedback by:

_____

_____

_____

_____

_____

_____

_____

How to nurture good feedback

Remember, for most people, criticizing (even in a constructive way) is a risky business. When people first do it, they will watch very closely to see what happens. The reaction received usually determines whether such feedback will be given again. You can avoid turning off future feedback by:

1. *Staying non-defensive. Listen — don't explain or justify.* Learn to bite your tongue. This is not the time to explain or justify actions even when we feel the criticism is unwarranted or stems from a misunderstanding. When you ask for feedback, the burden is on you to listen and try to understand. This does not mean you are obligated to believe or accept criticism, but try to understand why the other person feels and reacts the way he or she does.

   Defensiveness stifles the flow of feedback, for it tells the other person you are more interested in justifying yourself than in understanding him or her.

2. *Ask for more.* Especially in the open, verbal feedback process, there is an opportunity to get additional information. If you can honestly say, 'That's helpful, tell me more – is there anything else I should know about that?' this will encourage the continual flow of feedback.

3. *Express an honest reaction.* The person giving the feedback often wants to know your reaction to the data he or she has presented. The best guideline is to express your honest reaction. 'I'm a little surprised you said that but you probably have a point.' Or 'I'm not sure what to say. I never even thought of that, but I certainly will from now on.'

4. *Thank those who give you feedback and plan for the future.* Let people know that you realize how risky giving feedback can be and share your appreciation for their efforts. This might also be a good time to plan ahead for future feedback sessions, which should be less disturbing and more productive than the first one. Excellent leaders make this process a regular and ongoing one.

Now, having said all that about feedback, let me also say that not many people do this. Not because they wouldn't benefit from it but because they are afraid to. It takes a lot of guts not only to hear criticism but to actually fish for it! But then again there are many things most people would avoid to keep their heads comfortably buried in the sand.

The highly successful person is willing to do that which the unsuccessful person is not. Getting feedback which provides direction and control is a classic case of such an action. Dare to do it and you'll reap a rich reward.

Feedback checklist
Think back to the last time you received criticism from someone else. Did you:

- avoid defending or explaining yourself
  until the full criticism was expressed? ☐ yes ☐ no

- understand the criticizer's point of view as best you could? ☐ yes ☐ no
- ask for elaboration or clarification? ☐ yes ☐ no
- express an honest reaction? ☐ yes ☐ no
- thank the person for the feedback? ☐ yes ☐ no

Get to the point where you can answer yes to these questions and you'll receive a lot of useful feedback.

Block 4 – understanding planning

Planning is the fourth building block to successful life management. And it is critical to your success.

The nuts and bolts of time and task management

Time management experts agree that rule number one in the planning process is this: *use a planner*. I have designed a system called the 'Plan-it Life Organizer' (we illustrated sample 'Life Plan' worksheets earlier in Figures 2.1–2.3). In the next few pages, you will see other sample pages from the *Plan-it* in Figures 2.4–2.13. You may prefer to modify you own planner system or use another format.

How much time should we devote to daily planning? I recommend a minimum of 10 or 15 minutes a day solely devoted to planning. Use the steps described below and you'll see a significant boost in your personal effectiveness.

How to do effective daily task planning

Use the sample planner sheet on page 46 (Figure 2.5) to practise effective daily planning. Here are the steps.

1. *Develop a priority task list for each day.* This helps sort out the important tasks from the less important. Determine which tasks need to be attacked first, and which can be saved for later or dropped entirely.

   Here's the process: list in your planner the tasks you want to spend your time on that particular day.

   Your list might include items like 'complete the XYZ

report', 'get stamps', 'Billy's football game', 'eat more fish', or 'date' with your partner or one of the kids.

Don't be concerned with the importance of the items at this stage, just get in the habit of listing non-routine tasks that you'll want to do that day.

2. *Assign a letter priority to each item on the list.* Use A, B, C or *(asterisk). Put the letter A next to items that *must* be done. These are critical to you based on your values and goals. Tasks that are required, either by outside forces like your boss or by internal ones like your personal commitment, will normally receive an A priority. (In the Plan-it, you place the letter in the column right next to the item. Put the letter A for *must do* items.)

Use the letter B to indicate *should do* items. These are things that should be done, items that would really be worth spending some time on. They aren't quite as critical as the As, but are nevertheless important.

The letter C is used for *could do* items. These are things worth listing, worth thinking about. And if you get the As and Bs all done, worth doing.

The asterisk indicates an item that is *urgent* — something that must be done *now*. It is both important and time vital. You've got to get on it right away. The urgent task is not something planned during your dedicated planning time. It pops up and screams 'do me now!' When these come up, add them to your list, put an asterisk by them, and drop whatever else you're doing, even if it's an A item.

Caution: Use the asterisk sparingly. Be certain that an urgency is really important before you bump the rest of your plan to squeeze it in. Just because something makes a lot of noise doesn't mean it necessarily has to be done immediately. Don't let an apparent urgency override a planned *important* task.

Urgent items don't come up all that often. A, B and C items should cover most of your tasks.

3. *Assign a number to these tasks.* You can further sharpen your plan of attack — your strategy for getting your work done — by assigning a number to each task.

Use the numbering system as a chronological indicator. That is, ask which task can I realistically get at first? If I have a meeting at 2 pm and it's an A item, it may not be A-1, simply because there are other things I'll want to do earlier in the day. You decide how you use it, but the number system provides your marching orders.

Let's stop and do it ...
Assume that tomorrow is Monday. Go through the three steps listed on pages 43–5 and prioritize what you really need to do tomorrow (Figure 2.4). Include both business and personal tasks — especially those that tie in with your core values. Write your plan on page 46.

Figure 2.4 *A priority task-planner sheet*

plan·it _{life organizer}	Week of 19	This week		

A	Must do	✓	Completed
B	Should do	→	Moved
C	Could do	○	Delegated
✦	Urgent — DO NOW	✗	Deleted

Monday

Priority tasks	Schedule	Notes
	8	
	9	
	10	
	11	
	12	
	1	
	2	
	3	
	4	
	5	
		✓ Journal ⊔

Tuesday

Priority tasks	Schedule	Notes
	8	
	9	
	10	
	11	
	12	
	1	
	2	
	3	
	4	
	5	
		✓ Journal ⊔

Wednesday

Priority tasks	Schedule	Notes
	8	
	9	
	10	
	11	
	12	
	1	
	2	
	3	
	4	
	5	
		✓ Journal ⊔

Figure 2.5 *A sample planner sheet*

Completion symbols: the payoff
As you complete the tasks listed in your planner, you deserve a reward. This reward takes the form of a completion symbol.

Here are several completion symbols, starting with one that feels the best:

✓ The tick symbol indicates the task has been completed. That, my friends feels good. I prefer to put my tick marks all in red just to remind myself of just how productive I've been, and how colourful.

→ The second symbol, an arrow, is used when a task needs to be rescheduled, for whatever reason. Perhaps a meeting was postponed or an appointment changed, or the task simply could not be done because you were wrapped up in something else.

Note: Any time you use the arrow, be sure to reschedule the task to another day in the planner. When you reschedule the task for another day, you earn the right to forget about it for a while. It'll come up automatically on the new day you scheduled.

○ The third symbol used is to actually put in the margin to the left of the completion symbol column a circle, indicating that a task has been delegated to someone else.

It may be that you've asked your partner to pick up a book of stamps on the way home from work, or assigned Billy to clean out the garage before his football match. Or, it may be a more formal kind of delegation, where you've given a secretary, or another subordinate, a task to complete. If you have several people to whom you delegate, you may want to use the circle and put the initial of the person to whom the task is delegated inside the circle. When the task has been completed by that person, you then put a tick mark in the column.

X A fourth symbol is an X, which simply means that a task has been deleted. This may mean that you blew it and it just didn't get done, or it may mean that you've reconsidered and determined that this task simply isn't worth doing. Remember, you are in charge. If you schedule a task but later decide it really isn't what you want to do — so be it. You X it out.

Let's review the priority codes and completion symbols. What do the following mean?

A = _____

B = _____

C = _____

* = _____

✓ = _____

→ = _____

○ = _____

X = _____

Tying goals and values to your daily planning

Your priority task list provides a micro view of your daily activities. But how do these activities tie in with those long-term values and goals we've been talking about?

For most people they don't. And that's why people often fail to achieve what's really important to them. The challenge is to *make your daily activities consistent with your goals and values.*

In the *Plan-it Life Organizer* you'll find three sections which give it special power to help you be successful:

1. a monthly plan section
2. a yearly plan record
3. your life plan.

A sample of each of these pages is found in Figures 2.6–2.13 beginning on page 50. You may photocopy these for your personal use.

In doing your daily priority task planning, be sure that the goals and values you have articulated for yourself seep through. The 'Life Plan' section of a planner is a place where you record your core values and your value aligning activities for frequent reference. The more often you review these, the more likely they will become real for you. When doing your daily planning, don't forget to review 'the big picture' described in your life plan.

Likewise, your yearly plan and monthly plan should surface and become specific tasks on your daily activities. For example, let's say that your life plan indicates a high value placed on 'health and vigour'. You have then decided, as a value aligning activity, you're going to get involved in a regular programme of jogging. For your yearly plan record, one of your priority tasks for the year is that you're going to jog 500 miles.

You then translate that 500 miles jogging target into a task of jogging 60 miles this month. Put this goal on the monthly plan page. Since you have decided that you want to run 60 miles this month, you then need to translate that into daily activities. So your priority task now for a particular date may be to run three miles. Write that down, and in doing so, your values and long-term goals become daily tasks. You are focusing your energy on their completion.

Translate one of your core values into a daily activity using the following questionnaire. Write one of your core values in the top space. Then work down to daily activities.

- 'What are my lifetime goals?'   Core values   _____
- 'What do I want to accomplish this year ... every year?'   Yearly actions   _____
- 'What do I want to accomplish this month ... every month?'   Monthly actions   _____

- 'What do I want to accomplish this week ... every week?' Weekly actions _____
- 'What do I want to accomplish today to bring me more in line with my lifetime goal?' Daily actions _____

Plan-it forms

The following Figures 2.6–2.13 illustrate seven pages taken from the *Plan-it Life Organizer*. They may be copied for your personal use.

To be successful in the area of self-management you will require some sort of personal planner.

Figure 2.6 *The Plan-it Life Organizer*

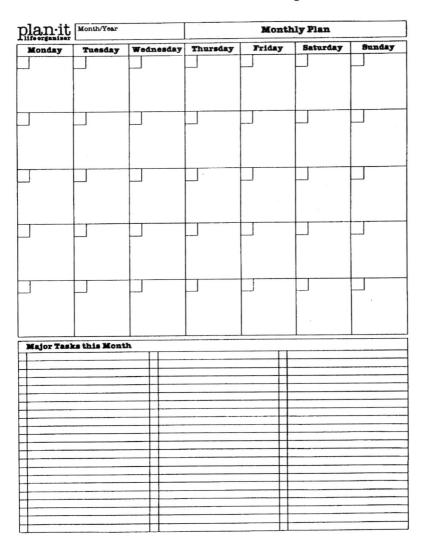

Figure 2.7 *The Plan-it Life Organizer (page 1)*

plan·it life organiser	Week of 19	This week
A Must do ✓ Completed		
B Should do → Moved		
C Could do O Delegated		
* Urgent—DO NOW x Deleted		

Monday

Priority tasks	Schedule	Notes
	8	
	9	
	10	
	11	
	12	
	1	
	2	
	3	
	4	
	5	
		✓ Journal ☐

Tuesday

Priority tasks	Schedule	Notes
	8	
	9	
	10	
	11	
	12	
	1	
	2	
	3	
	4	
	5	
		✓ Journal ☐

Wednesday

Priority tasks	Schedule	Notes
	8	
	9	
	10	
	11	
	12	
	1	
	2	
	3	
	4	
	5	
		✓ Journal ☐

Figure 2.8 *The Plan-it Life Organizer (page 2)*

Thursday

Priority tasks	Schedule	Notes
	8	
	9	
	10	
	11	
	12	
	1	
	2	
	3	
	4	
	5	
		✓ Journal ☐

Friday

Priority tasks	Schedule	Notes
	8	
	9	
	10	
	11	
	12	
	1	
	2	
	3	
	4	
	5	
		✓ Journal ☐

Saturday

Priority tasks	Schedule	Notes
		✓ Journal ☐

Sunday

Priority tasks	Schedule	Notes
		✓ Journal ☐

Figure 2.9 *The Plan-it Life Organizer (page 3)*

plan·it _{life organiser}	Year	Yearly Plan/Record	

January	February	March

April	May	June

July	August	September

October	November	December

Figure 2.10 *The Plan-it Life Organizer (page 4)*

plan·it life organizer	Year	Priority Tasks this Year

Figure 2.11 *The Plan-it Life Organizer (page 5)*

plan·it life organiser	Year		Priority Tasks this Year

Figure 2.12 *The Plan-it Life Organizer (page 6)*

plan·it	Life Plan
life organizer	

Core Values	Value Aligning Activities

Figure 2.13   *The Plan-it Life Organizer (page 7)*

Block 5 – understanding productivity

The last 'P' of our success building blocks is *'productivity'*. Listed below are the six most common productivity killers. In the box next to each, list two or three defences against it. On page 59 you will find suggestions on some other ideas you may not have thought of.

Productivity killer	What do you do to defend against this killer?
1. Interruptions Is this a problem for you? ☐ yes ☐ no	_____
2. Clutter and paperwork Is this a problem for you? ☐ yes ☐ no	_____
3. Unproductive communication Is this a problem for you? ☐ yes ☐ no	_____
4. Procrastination Is this a problem for you? ☐ yes ☐ no	_____
5. Indecision Is this a problem for you? ☐ yes ☐ no	_____
6. Self-overload Is this a problem for you? ☐ yes ☐ no	_____

Some time-tested defences against the big six productivity killers

1. Interruptions

Assertively decline to be interrupted
The next time someone asks, 'Hey, got a minute?' you may be wise to gather up your most assertive skills — that doesn't mean being abusive or abrasive, but simply being assertive — and say, 'Gosh, I really don't. I'm in the middle of something right now. Could I get back to you in about 20 minutes?'

Do you think anyone would be offended by an approach like this? It's unlikely. But even if they are, the appropriate use of your time is more important than their momentary pique. Occasionally offering small offence to overly sensitive people is a small price to pay for greater effectiveness and satisfaction.

The most important way of avoiding unproductive interruptions is simply to *decline to be interrupted.* Tell people that you're working on something right now and that you'd be glad to talk with them later.

Let people know when interruptions are okay
Schedule particular blocks of time that are open for people to come and visit you with their concerns. Scheduling such time on your *Plan-it*, and coordinating it with your secretary, is a useful way of letting people know that they can come in with problems they have during those hours. Then stick to those hours.

Respect other people's time
Don't interrupt others unless absolutely necessary. Always check with people to be sure they are not in the middle of an A priority. When calling on the phone ask, 'Do you have a minute to talk about this now?' before launching into the topic of your call. By doing so, you send another unspoken message that you value time — theirs and your own.

While you are thinking about interruptions, write at least

one action idea you intend to apply to stop this productivity killer:

_____

_____

_____

2. Clutter and paperwork

Handle each paper only once
Learn to make decisions — not just postponing actions — on each letter, memo or document you receive.

Usually you have four options:

F — file it for future reference.
R — refer it to someone else.
A — act on it — now!
T — trash it.

Studies show that 95 per cent of the stuff in files for more than one year will never be used. Periodically clean out those files so that your system stays lean and efficient. When in doubt, throw it out. Get a handle on the kind of information you need to keep and get rid of the rest. Don't get bogged down in sheer quantity of stuff cluttering your life.

How to 'read' a magazine
As you read magazines, clip or tear out items that are important to you. Set aside these articles, advertisements or other items that you may want to refer to in the future. _Do not keep the entire magazine._ Keeping the whole magazine simply adds to the clutter in your life.

By the way, about 75 per cent of a magazine is advertising or information you don't need.

While you are thinking about clutter and paperwork, write at least one action idea you intend to apply to stop this productivity killer:

_____

_____

_____

3. Unproductive communication

Choose the right media for your message
Don't send a letter when a phone call will do. Don't make a call when a personal visit is needed (even if the visit takes more time and energy). Communication *efficiency* is simply a matter of 'reaching' the most people at the lowest cost. Memos, posters and mass meetings can do that. Communication *effectiveness*, however, means reaching the right people with the right message in a timely and useful form. Often this means one-to-one conversations, small group discussions and the like. Effective communication media almost always costs more than efficient media. Many people, however, fail to count the costs of the backlash when efficient media is used inappropriately (such as a mass announcement of an issue that should have been handled personally).

Keep getting feedback
Even 'simple' instruction-giving should be accompanied with feedback. Always give the person you are talking to the opportunity to question and clarify. A few extra moments spent now can save hours of 'fixing' later.

Keep your boss appraised of your priorities
A five-minute planning meeting each day can clear the air and improve organizational productivity.
   If your boss doesn't seem to be too open to such a meeting, try this. Each day, give your boss a brief memo saying something like this:

Dear Big Boss,
Here's what I'm going to be doing today. I've assigned my A-1 priority to finishing the Murphy report. When I'm finished with that, my A-2 priority is getting together the data for the budget [etc].

If these priorities are not consistent with what you need me to be doing, please let me know. If I do not hear from you, I will assume that I'm on the right track.

A simple memo like that provides effective communication and coordination.

While you are thinking about unproductive communication, write at least one action idea you intend to apply to stop this productivity killer:

_____

_____

4. Procrastination

- Some experts say there are just three reasons for procrastination: fear of failure, fear of success or the desire to rebel against 'the system'. Determine which reason you are using when you procrastinate a task.
- Use your daily priority task list found in your planner.
- Do the worst task first. Get it over with and enjoy the rest of the day.
- Make dreaded tasks into games. Compete against others or yourself. Try to beat your last effort. Play mind games.
- Discipline (sorry, but ultimately it may come down to that).

While you are thinking about procrastination, write at least one action idea you intend to apply to stop this productivity killer. (Do this now, not later.)

_____

_____

5. Indecision

- Successful people are seeing the value in the simple three-word motto, *ready–fire–aim*. Think through your idea (get ready), try it (fire!), and observe/correct the results needed (aim). Wal-Mart founder Sam Walton bought into this approach when he constantly challenged his people to try out new ideas, not just mull them over in their minds. Get yourself *doing something* and then adjust the aim as necessary.
- Avoid 'perfection paralysis'. Everything you do won't be right, but start with 'rough draft' and shape and improve as you go.
- Decide to be more decisive. Make your decisions and stick to them so long as they still make good sense.

While you are thinking about indecision, write at least one action idea you intend to apply to stop this productivity killer:

_____

_____

6. Self-overload

- I've talked throughout this book of ways of focusing your energy on things that are important — the value-based things that are important to you. A constant focus on the valuable is critical to reducing the problem of self-overload. If a task doesn't add value in some way, don't do it.
- Delegate all you can, not just what you want to. Be creative in seeking ways to double up your efforts with other people's. Offer to help when they need it and they'll be there for you.
- Put your major efforts into your value-based activities. (The other stuff isn't as important.)
- Stay flexible. Don't become a time nut. Someone described a time nut as one who got so programmed that he missed a

slot in a revolving door and it threw him off-stride for a whole week.

If you get off-stride, if you forget to use the planner for a day or two, or if you forget to use some of these other techniques, don't worry about it. Just step back and start over again. But once you develop the habit of using these tools, you'll find that you'll achieve a stress-reduced balance in your life (Figure 2.14).

Don't become a robot. Understand the nature of time and these principles of self-management but stay flexible.

Decision guide

When deciding how to use your time, ask:

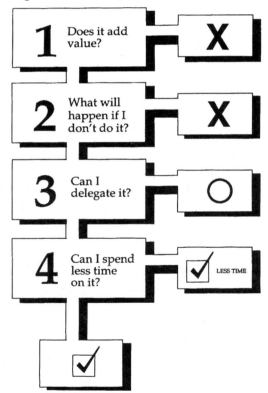

Figure 2.14 *A decision guide*

CHAPTER 3

A Final Thought About Balance in Your Life

CASE STUDY

Tony's story:

Tony sure looked successful. He was a young executive with a fast-growing company. His work seemed exciting. He travelled quite a bit (always first class), earned a salary that put him in the top 10 per cent of wage earners nationally. He drove a sporty car, wore an expensive watch and dressed sharply. He was the kind of guy a lot of college students aspired to become. He had made it.

And he was miserable.

Under the thin veneer of success lived a basically unhappy man — a fellow travelling life's fast lane with a seriously lopsided wheel. Tony's only problem was one of balance.

His career had become his whole life. He loved his job and dedicated himself to it with a vengeance. But after work, there wasn't much else to life. Tony was single and had no regular companionship with people who cared about him away from the office. His family lived halfway across the country; he was a member of no civic organization, no church, no nothing. His job was his life.

Lots of people fall into the lopsided wheel trap. We get

wrapped up in some aspect of our life (career, children, church work, civic involvement, physical training, politics, whatever) so deeply that nothing else is significant. We become compulsively one-sided.

Wellness and centring a lopsided wheel

How do we achieve a sense of wellness – a social and psychological as well as a physical sense of well-being? A centred wheel can help (Figure 3.1).

Visualize an old-fashioned wheel with spokes. If the spokes are all about the same length, the wheel is balanced. If not, we're talking bumpy ride.

Everyone's wheel has a different number of spokes. The minimum number is three, representing values such as:

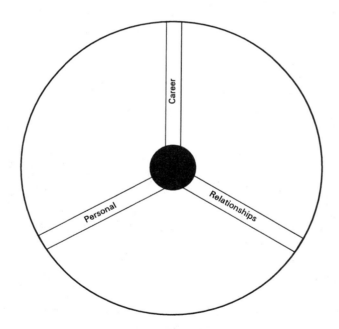

Figure 3.1 *A centred three-spoke wheel representing personal life, relationships and career*

- our *personal* life (including our sense of growth, spiritual dimensions and psychological and physical well-being)
- our *relationships* (including the well-being of our family, friendships and rewarding social involvement)
- our *career* (or vocation: the efforts we make to produce or create something of value and receive the rewards associated with that).

Some people envision wheels with more spokes, like the one shown in Figure 3.2. Each spoke represents a growth dimension of life – sources of satisfaction or dissatisfaction. Use your own core values as spokes. For example, yours might include:

- physical
- mental
- career/financial

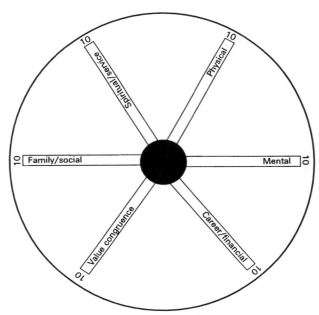

Figure 3.2 *A centred six-spoke wheel representing a growth dimension of life*

- spiritual/service
- family/social
- value congruence.

The centred wheel on page 67 is an example of good life balance. Each spoke on the wheel is calibrated from 0 to 10, representing your *degree of satisfaction* with the *progress* you are making towards value congruence. A 1 reflects extreme dissatisfaction; a 10, a feeling of great satisfaction.

A lopsided wheel: an example

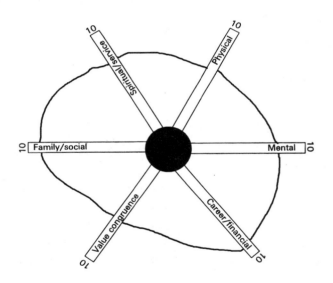

Figure 3.3 *A lopsided wheel*

The wheel shown in Figure 3.3 is an example of a lopsided wheel. Although spokes such as family/social and career/financial suggest feelings of rather high satisfaction, other spokes, like value congruence, indicate areas of lesser satisfaction. The lopsided wheel helps show you specifically what areas to work on to reach a better balance.

Is your wheel round or lopsided?

Now determine your own state of life balance (Figure 3.4). Label each of your spokes from one to ten. Then draw a line connecting the points on each spoke. Is your wheel lopsided? Is it square? Is something sticking out too far?

Look at the short spokes and determine what can be done to boost your satisfaction with those aspects of your life.

Redraw your wheel every month or so. (An extra copy is found in Figure 3.5.) By doing so, you can achieve a sense of balance — the feeling that comes from using time and resources to gain satisfaction in the areas that are critical to whole person wellness. That is the essence of successful self-management.

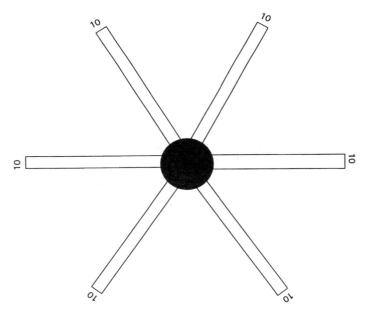

Figure 3.4 *Your balance wheel (1)*

Your balance wheel

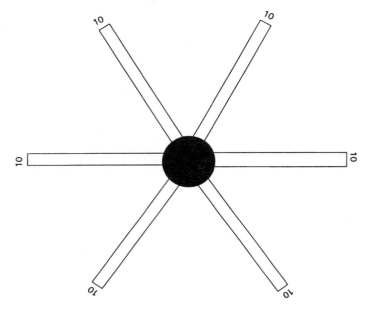

Figure 3.5 *Your balance wheel (2)*

Rate the progress you are making towards congruence with your core values. Name each spoke and then rate yourself from 0 to 10. Feel free to add additional spokes to represent other values. Then draw the wheel connecting your spots on each spoke. Do this every few months in a different colour ink to see what kind of progress you are making.

Further Reading

Brown, Melanie (1987) *Attaining Personal Greatness*, William Morrow and Co, New York), p. 17.

Locke, Edwin A and Latham, Gary P (1984) *Goal Setting: A Motivational Technique That Works!* Prentice-Hall, Inc Englewood Cliffs, NJ: quotes from dustcover.

For two excellent books on this subject consider ordering *Preventing Job Burnout* by Dr Beverly A Potter, and *Balancing Home and Career* by Pam Conrad.

Thomas, J Peters and Waterman, Robert A Jr (1982) *In Search of Excellence*, Random House, New York.

Notes